What Was the March on Washington?

by Kathleen Krull

illustrated by Tim Tomkinson

Penguin Workshop

To all my librarian friends—KK

For Parker and Chase—TT

PENGUIN WORKSHOP
An Imprint of Penguin Random House LLC, New York

Text copyright © 2013 by Kathleen Krull. Illustrations copyright © 2013 by Tim Tomkinson. All rights reserved. Published by Penguin Workshop, an imprint of Penguin Random House LLC, New York. PENGUIN and PENGUIN WORKSHOP are trademarks of Penguin Books Ltd. WHO HQ & Design is a registered trademark of Penguin Random House LLC.
Printed in the USA.

Visit us online at www.penguinrandomhouse.com.

Library of Congress Control Number: 2012031483

ISBN 9780448462875   30 29 28 27 26 25 24 23 22 21 20

Contents

What Was the March on Washington? 1

Separate and Not Equal 5

The Power of Marches 26

JFK 36

No Detail Too Small 42

A Crowd Gathers and Gathers 56

Millions of Footsteps 70

The Power of Words 79

"We Shall Overcome" 93

Timelines 102

Bibliography 104

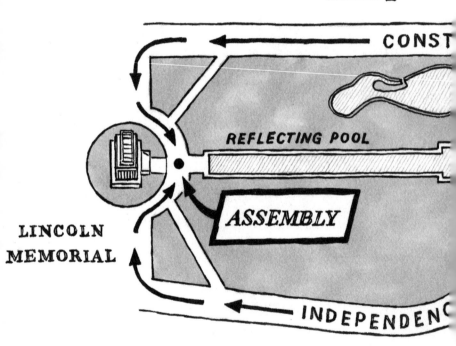

Bus Parking
ZONE *3*
ZONE *1*

CONST

REFLECTING POOL

ASSEMBLY

LINCOLN
MEMORIAL

INDEPENDENC

Bus Parking
ZONE *2*

The Route of the Marchers

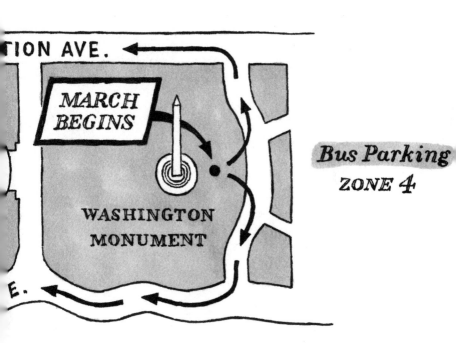

What Was the March on Washington?

A quarter of a million Americans streamed into Washington, DC, from all parts of the country. They came by bus, on trains, in cars, and on motorcycles.

Some people walked from New York City, a 230-mile trip that took eleven days. One man even roller-skated. They all came in support of a single cause: equal rights for black Americans. By gathering together, they were shining light on the terrible problem of racism in the United States.

What is racism? Racism in America is the belief among some white people that they are better than black people. Smarter, too. It is the belief that black people do not deserve the same rights that white people have.

Despite threats of violence

in Washington, people, both young and old and black and white, came to the city. They marched, sang, and listened to speeches, including a very famous one by Martin Luther King Jr., one of the most famous in history.

At the time, it was the largest protest ever held in America. It led to real changes in our laws and how African Americans lived their lives.

It was called the March on Washington for Jobs and Freedom, and it took place on the steamy afternoon of August 28, 1963. The March was held in Washington, DC, because it is the US capital, a city that represents everyone in the country. It is where Congress meets to pass laws. And it is home to the beautiful Lincoln Memorial, which honors the president who helped bring slavery to an end.

CHAPTER 1
Separate and Not Equal

Slavery ended for African Americans in 1865 after the Civil War. But being set free and being treated as equals to white people are not the same thing.

In 1963, almost one hundred years later, blacks still lived lives that were far from equal to whites' lives. Nearly nineteen million African Americans lived in the United States, making up about 10 to 12 percent of the US population. But states and cities had many ways of keeping the races apart, or segregating them.

In the South, the rules separating blacks from whites were called Jim Crow laws. The name was popularized by a stage show in the 1800s in which a white performer in blackface makeup sang a song about a silly black man named Jim Crow.

The Jim Crow laws said that blacks couldn't buy houses in certain neighborhoods. They had to live in less desirable areas. Their public bathrooms were separate, as were sections in theaters and drinking fountains. Some fountains labeled COLORED did not even have cool water.

African Americans weren't allowed to try on clothes before buying them. Certain public swimming pools and amusement parks were off-limits to them, as were certain restaurants and diners.

Birmingham, Alabama, even banned blacks and whites from playing card games together, as well as "dice, dominoes, checkers, baseball, softball, football, basketball, or similar games."

In the South, schools and colleges were segregated. So were hospitals, orphanages, funeral homes, cemeteries, and all forms of public transportation. On buses, blacks could only sit in the back and had to give up their seats if white people wanted them. Conditions were better for blacks in the North, but by custom and practice, the races were still mostly segregated there, too.

Special laws made it difficult for blacks to vote and elect people who would fight for their rights. For instance, in Alabama, black people had to take a reading test with tricky questions before they could sign up to vote. White people didn't have to do this.

In 1963, it was still against the law in twenty-one states for a white and black couple to get married.

Thurgood Marshall

A Landmark Case:
Brown v. Board of Education

A third-grader was at the heart of a case that overturned segregation in public schools. Linda Brown of Topeka, Kansas, lived near an all-white school but had to take a bus to an all-black school that was much farther away and not as good. Her father and twelve other parents sued the Topeka Board of Education. The case went all the way to the Supreme Court. Thurgood Marshall, who later became the first black Supreme Court Justice, argued for integrating the schools. And in a unanimous decision in 1954, the court ruled that segregation in public schools was illegal. *Separate*, by definition, could not be the same as *equal*. After this, separating the races came under attack in other areas of life in America. And civil rights leaders asked: Could other branches of the government do even more to help?

In 1963, America seemed to be split into two different countries. Separate and definitely not equal.

The jobs open to blacks were usually low paying: maid, janitor, dishwasher, driver, garbage collector, cotton picker, and tobacco field hand. On TV and in the movies, blacks were portrayed in these same roles.

Professional sports teams were segregated, too. Modern Major League Baseball teams were all white until Jackie Robinson joined the Brooklyn Dodgers in 1947. He had to promise the team owner he would take insults in silence and ignore hate mail and death threats.

What could happen if a black person disobeyed the Jim Crow laws?

In 1955, fourteen-year-old Emmett Till was beaten to death because he may have whistled at a white woman.

And then there was lynching. A lynching was

a public hanging that could be imposed for any offense, even an imaginary one. The body would often be left dangling for others to see. Between 1882 and 1963, almost 3,500 blacks were lynched.

The Ku Klux Klan

The KKK was a powerful, secretive terrorist group formed by six Confederate soldiers soon after the South lost the Civil War. Though they also hated Catholics, Jews, immigrants, and other groups, members were mainly white supremacists. They believed the white race to be superior to the black. They had secret handshakes and passwords, took odd titles (like Grand Wizard), and wore white pointy hats and sheets to disguise their identities and frighten their victims. They enforced Jim Crow laws and terrorized blacks by setting crosses on fire on families' front lawns, burning houses, and bombing churches. They beat up people. They lynched people, too.

At its peak in the 1920s, the KKK had about four million members. In 2012, the Klan still had over five thousand members, mostly in the South.

Without any basic civil rights, it was almost impossible for blacks to fight back. This was "normal" life, and it didn't appear that it would ever change.

But by the 1950s, brave African Americans were starting to fight—not with their fists, but through actions that said they were fed up with being treated this way. This kind of protest is called nonviolent civil disobedience. The protesters were deliberately disobeying laws in ways that didn't use violence.

For instance, groups of black college students would sit at "white" lunch counters in different southern cities. They knew they wouldn't be served. But they sat quietly and behaved politely. Most often, the sit-ins ended when police came and dragged them off to jail.

It wasn't just young black people who protested. In 1955, a middle-aged seamstress named Rosa Parks was arrested in Montgomery, Alabama. She had refused to give up her seat on a public bus to a white person.

Rosa Parks

Right after that, a young preacher, Dr. Martin Luther King Jr., told the black people of Montgomery, Alabama, to boycott public buses. They should stop riding them and find other ways to get around. The bus boycott lasted more than a year. And it worked. The Supreme Court finally outlawed segregated buses in 1956. For his part in the boycott, King now emerged as a strong national leader.

The Importance of Churches

Churches were where many blacks gathered their courage to fight back. Since the 1800s, blacks had been breaking away from white churches and forming their own, such as the African Methodist Episcopal (AME) Church. At church, they strengthened their identities and learned how to organize, recruit, and raise funds for protests and bailing protesters out of jail. It was no accident that many civil rights leaders, such as Martin Luther King Jr., were preachers or ministers.

The hottest spot in 1963 was Birmingham, Alabama. King wrote, "Birmingham is probably the most thoroughly segregated city in the United States." Sometimes it was called "Bombingham." More than fifty bombs had been set off in black homes and churches in the previous twenty years. In May 1963, King and others organized a children's march in which children—some as

young as six years old—hoped to speak to the mayor of Birmingham about ending segregation. That never happened. Instead, hundreds of students were arrested and jailed.

Scenes of cruelty were broadcast on TV. While white adults threw bricks and bottles at the young marchers, the police turned on high-pressure water hoses, the kind used to put out fires. Kids

were lifted clear into the air and slammed to the pavement or into buildings. Then the police brought out snarling attack dogs. Many kids thought they were about to die, and several had to be hospitalized.

As nothing else had before, the TV images showed viewers all over the country what life was like for blacks in the South. One black minister named Fred Shuttlesworth said, "The whole world is watching Birmingham."

Nineteen sixty-three was heating to a boil. Civil rights protests were taking place in many different areas, but not on a national level.

It was time for many people to speak with one voice on a national stage . . . in Washington, DC.

The White House

CHAPTER 2
The Power of Marches

A. Philip Randolph, a man long active in the movement to get blacks their civil rights under the law, understood the power of marches.

Just before World War II, he had planned a march in Washington to protest the absence of blacks in the defense industry, which provided well-paying jobs making things like planes, submarines, and warships. But before the march took place, President Franklin D. Roosevelt met Randolph's demands. Why? First Lady Eleanor Roosevelt was a strong supporter of civil rights. She put pressure on her husband. FDR made it illegal to not hire blacks for defense-industry jobs.

Randolph again planned to lead a big march in 1948. He hoped to call attention to the fact that the US Army, Navy, and Marines all treated blacks unfairly. Harry Truman was president by then. Just as FDR had done, Truman headed off this march. He signed orders guaranteeing equal opportunities for all races in the military.

Randolph's focus had always been on better jobs and better pay for blacks. This went all the way back to his years with the Brotherhood of Sleeping Car Porters. By the 1920s, being a porter—taking care of overnight passengers on train trips—was one of the best-paying jobs open to black men. Yet Randolph saw how unfairly black porters were treated, so he founded the Brotherhood. It was the first time that African Americans had a real labor union, a group speaking on the behalf of all its workers. In 1937, after twelve years of struggling for better pay, the union of black porters threatened to go on strike,

or stop working. As a result their wages were doubled and job conditions improved.

In 1963, A. Philip Randolph was seventy-four years old. But he was still gutsy and full of passion for civil rights. He wanted a march to *actually* take place—and on the biggest possible scale.

Randolph reached out with letters and phone calls to those in his network of religious leaders as well as ordinary people. Above all, to make the March happen, he would need the cooperation of all the major civil rights leaders.

At first, Randolph got little response from the other leaders, including Martin Luther King Jr. They were busy with their own projects. But Randolph wouldn't take no for an answer and kept nudging.

A. Philip Randolph

Bayard Rustin

While he wooed the leaders, Randolph turned to someone else to work out all the details of the March: Bayard Rustin, who was known as a total genius at organizing. He had been working for civil rights for thirty years.

Born in 1912, Rustin had grown up in West Chester, Pennsylvania. He was a man with strong beliefs. He did not believe in violence—ever. So he did not believe in war, even a war for a good cause. For his refusal to fight in World War II, he served two and a half years in jail. He was most influenced by Mohandas Gandhi. Gandhi was the leader who freed India from British rule. How did he do it? Not by telling people to take up arms and fight the British, but by nonviolence—peaceful resistance. In 1948, India became an independent country. Rustin traveled there to learn more about nonviolence from Gandhi's followers.

Later, Rustin became a big influence on Martin Luther King Jr. He believed in peaceful protests, too. Bayard Rustin even helped King with some of his speeches.

Important Civil Rights Groups in the U.S.A.

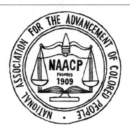

NAACP stands for the National Association for the Advancement of Colored People. Founded in 1909, it is the nation's oldest civil rights group. One of its aims was to end lynching. This group prefers to use the legal system to bring about change.

CORE is the Congress of Racial Equality, founded in 1942. Members of the organization believe in nonviolent action, such as Freedom Rides.

SCLC, the Southern Christian Leadership Conference, was established after the successful Montgomery bus boycott. Martin Luther King Jr. was its first president.

SNCC (the Student Nonviolent Coordinating Committee) was started in 1960 by college students and other young people. Its members hoped to force change through sit-ins, Freedom Rides, and other protests.

CHAPTER 3
JFK

A. Philip Randolph had another ally in the civil rights cause: John F. Kennedy. He was the first Catholic president of the United States. JFK understood what it felt like to be the target of prejudice. When he ran for office in 1960, he spoke about his hope for a United States of America "where no one cares what color your skin is."

Three months after he won the election—by a very narrow margin—JFK was sending his first package of civil rights laws to Congress, laws that were promptly watered down by his opponents. Behind the scenes, his brother Robert, the attorney general, was warning him that the federal government—not the states—had to do something about segregation or the country could fall into chaos.

Robert F. Kennedy

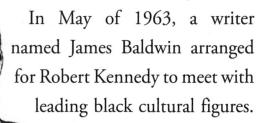

In May of 1963, a writer named James Baldwin arranged for Robert Kennedy to meet with leading black cultural figures. He listened carefully as they warned of how out of touch the government was, and then reported back to his brother.

On June 11, 1963, JFK gave one of the most important civil rights speeches a president had ever delivered. Millions watched on prime-time TV. He declared, "The time has come for this nation to fulfill its promise" to make all citizens "fully free." He added, "Race has no place in American lives or in American law."

Eight days later, JFK presented to Congress the Civil Rights Act of 1963. It called for the government to make certain that blacks could vote, attend integrated public schools, be served in public places, and have the chance for decent jobs. Basic human rights.

JFK urged Congress to pass the bill quickly, for many reasons, "but, above all, because it is right." The battle was going to be straight uphill: There were no black senators and just five black members of the House of Representatives.

Randolph had been planning the March for months, but JFK's civil rights bill sped up his timetable. The March on Washington had to happen very quickly. On July 2, he announced that it would take place on August 28.

It was to be peaceful and huge, with a goal of at least one hundred thousand marchers, blacks and whites together—a "living petition" for the passage of JFK's bill. Randolph brought about a rare display of unity among civil rights leaders. In the end, all of them respected Randolph so much, they agreed to make the March work.

Most congressmen, even the people who were for civil rights, didn't believe a march would help pass JFK's bill. A senator from South Carolina warned that "criminal . . . elements, as well as crackpots, will move in to take every advantage of this mob."

Many people worried about violence. Controlling a crowd that large was going to be very difficult, especially on a hot summer day. Antiblack groups like the American Nazi Party were threatening to show up to protest. To them, civil rights meant "the end of America, it is the end of the white race."

Even JFK did not approve of the March at first. He argued with the March's leaders. "Some of these people [in Congress] are looking for an excuse to be against us; and I don't want to give any of them a chance to say, 'Yes, I'm for the bill, but I am damned if I will vote for it at the point of a gun.'" Of course, the marchers would not be carrying guns. What JFK meant was that people don't like to be forced into anything. He thought some members of Congress might view the March as forcing them to vote for the civil rights bill.

Randolph and Rustin remained calm and focused.

Yes, the risks were high, but this march was going to be a thrilling step forward for the black people of the United States.

They went full-steam ahead with their plans.

CHAPTER 4
No Detail Too Small

Bayard Rustin had only two months to plan what was intended to be the largest peaceful demonstration in American history.

His job was to organize a protest on a gigantic scale—without cell phones, computers, the Internet, or much of the technology we take for granted today.

Within days he had a tentative plan and a core staff of volunteers. They would be in charge of other volunteers around the country. Both his small office in Washington and the main headquarters in the New York City neighborhood of Harlem received bomb threats every day.

Rustin doodled on his yellow legal pad, his brain going a mile a minute. Within two weeks he

Segregated water fountains

A classroom in an all-black school in the South

A classroom in an all-white school in the South

Thurgood Marshall

In 1954, after a landmark Supreme Court case, Linda Brown (far left) was able to attend a school that used to be for white children only.

Segregationists protesting integration

President John F. Kennedy with members of the NAACP

Firefighters hosing civil rights protesters in Birmingham, Alabama

John Lewis addressing marchers

NATIONAL HEADQUARTERS

MARCH
ON
WASHINGTON
FOR JOBS & FREEDOM
WED. AUG. 28

Bayard Rustin (left) with civil
rights leader Cleveland Robinson

A. Philip Randolph (left) and Roy Wilkins
(center), planning the route of the March with
civil rights leader Anna Arnold Hedgeman

Leaders of the March in front of the Lincoln Memorial

A packed crowd at the March

Images of
the March

Demonstrators dipping their feet into the reflecting pool

Martin Luther King Jr. delivering his "I Have a Dream" speech

The National Mall and the Washington Monument

President Lyndon B. Johnson signing the Civil Rights Act (1964),
as Martin Luther King Jr. and others look on

had a manual and sent it to two thousand leaders, white and black. It laid detailed groundwork for getting a huge turnout on such short notice. It was "a call for action"—setting up transportation committees, ways to make the March known, and ways to raise funds. It called for captains aboard every bus, train, and plane.

The March was going to cost about $135,000. His staff went after donations from churches, organizations, and individuals. They raised about two-thirds of the money this way. They also sold souvenirs—many thousands of buttons showing a black hand and a white hand clasped together. They held fund-raising

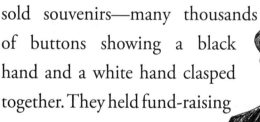

concerts, or hootenannies, with folksingers like Joan Baez and a new, gravel-voiced singer named Bob Dylan.

Rustin worked as if he were putting together a huge ad campaign for a new product. The flyers his team mailed out began with the words "An Appeal to You." They sent as many as one hundred thousand a day, with local phone numbers to call to sign up. There were spots on radio and

TV, interviews on TV talk shows, newspaper and magazine ads, concerts, and rallies. Rustin contacted Hollywood celebrities, who used their star power to get out the word.

The day chosen for the March was a Wednesday. It needed to be on a weekday. Why? Church groups were planning to come in big numbers. But church groups wouldn't skip their Sunday services.

Reverend Abraham Woods said, "If we didn't have the crowd, it would be perceived that we would've flunked." Rustin's organizers went to all the major cities to work closely with local leaders to do the hard work of signing up marchers and getting them to Washington. In all, some fifteen hundred groups across the country helped.

How to get all those people to the capital? Cars were discouraged as parking would be limited. So Rustin's team began lining up enough buses and trains.

How would they keep people comfortable? Memos advised marchers to wear low-heeled shoes and to each bring sunglasses, a hat, and a raincoat. Marchers could bring portable stools, and hundreds of folding chairs were to be supplied for the elderly.

What about food? It was okay to bring picnic baskets, box lunches, and thermos bottles of water, but no alcohol. The recommended sandwich was peanut butter and jelly. Sandwiches with mayo were not good; they could go bad in the heat. Churches were encouraged to

donate lunches. One New York church packed up eighty thousand cheese sandwiches, apples, and slices of marble cake. Hot dogs and other food would be sold, with large coolers of soda donated by the Coca-Cola Company.

Some twenty portable drinking fountains were rented.

Bathrooms and first aid? Rustin arranged for nearly three hundred portable "Johnny-on-the-spot" toilets. He planned to set up twenty-two first-aid stations with forty doctors and eighty nurses on hand.

What route should the marchers take? They were not going to pass by Congress on Capitol Hill or the White House. This was a march about freedom, not politics. Instead, they would walk along the National Mall between two landmarks, from the Washington Monument to the Lincoln Memorial. These monuments were connected by a reflecting pool almost a half mile long and a vast lawn. From the steps of the Lincoln Memorial, speakers would address the crowd.

Rustin planned an afternoon of inspiring speeches by handpicked speakers. He soothed the egos of those not chosen. Speeches had to be approved in advance and could last no longer than five minutes.

Rustin wanted the best sound system available so the speakers' voices would carry clearly for one square mile, otherwise the crowd wouldn't pay attention. Along the Mall, miles of wires were laid to carry telephone, television, and radio lines.

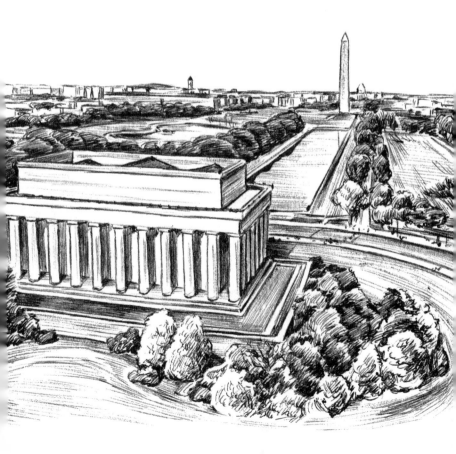

Signs of Protest

Marchers were given preprinted signs with Rustin-approved messages in red and blue letters. With the most frequent word being "now," some typical signs said:

I AM A MAN

WE DEMAND VOTING RIGHTS NOW

WE DEMAND DECENT HOUSING NOW

GRADUALLY ISN'T FAST ENOUGH

WE DEMAND JOBS NOW!

FREEDOM IN '63

Some unapproved signs read:

MY NAME IS CHARLIE JONES, MR. KENNEDY, AND I CAN'T WAIT (carried by a nine-year-old boy)

NO MATTER HOW YOU POLISH IT, SEGREGATION IS DIRTY, ROTTEN, EVIL

HORSES HAVE THEIR OWN TELEVISION SHOWS. DOGS HAVE THEIR OWN TELEVISION SHOWS. WHY CAN'T NEGROES HAVE THEIR OWN SHOWS?

A big concern was how to keep marchers safe. Rustin worked with Washington's police chief. A vast security force was on standby: 8,900 policemen, firemen, National Guard and army members, and marines. In case of a riot, they were armed with guns, clubs, and toxic tear gas. Thirty helicopters were also on standby, sent to Washington from Fort Bragg. Washington's main hospital had a disaster plan ready.

In addition, Rustin assembled a team of unarmed marshals. They were taught how to control a crowd without force. Also, there would be leaders on every bus to explain to passengers what to do if someone insulted or hit them. They were to ignore it and *not* fight back. They should leave it to the marshals to respond. There were to be *no* acts of civil disobedience that could lead to arrest.

Over five hundred cameramen, technicians, and reporters were to be on hand—with more cameras than had filmed the last presidential inauguration.

For a month, the president remained silent about the historic event about to take place in the capital. Finally, on July 17, President Kennedy spoke at a press conference in support of the March. Later, he declined to speak at it, but agreed to meet with the leaders that day.

By mid-August, there were no more buses

available to rent on the East Coast. All scheduled planes, trains, and buses were filled to capacity.

The Mall was filled with the sounds of carpenters hammering nails into the speakers' platform on the steps of the Lincoln Memorial.

Then, on the night before, someone damaged the sound system. Luckily US Army sound engineers were able to fix it, working through the night.

Up in his hotel room, Martin Luther King Jr. also worked all through the night—on his speech.

The question was: How many people would show up to hear it?

CHAPTER 5
A Crowd Gathers and Gathers

At 6:00 a.m. on the big day, reporters hassled Bayard Rustin, wanting to know where the marchers were. He looked down at his yellow legal pad and assured them, "Gentlemen, everything is going exactly according to plan."

The aide next to him could see that the paper was blank.

It was still dark when the first bus came. Thirty-eight high-energy students from Mississippi got off.

Trains started arriving at 7:25. One of them had eight hundred teenagers on board.

There were rumors that local residents were sitting on their porches with loaded guns.

"People were afraid," said one witness. "We didn't know what we would meet."

In fact, many residents had left the city, fearing riots. Fewer than half of the government workers in the city showed up to their jobs that Wednesday.

By midmorning, a train was pulling into Union Station every ten minutes. Every hour, one hundred buses passed through the Baltimore Harbor Tunnel on the way to DC.

Chatting quietly, throngs of people surged toward the Washington Monument. They picked up signs and programs that listed the speakers. They bought buttons that said "I Was There."

MARCH ON WASHINGTON FOR JOBS AND FREEDOM
AUGUST 28, 1963

LINCOLN MEMORIAL PROGRAM

1.	The National Anthem	*Led By* Marian Anderson
2.	Invocation	The Rev. Patrick O'Doyle
3.	Opening Remarks	A. Philip Randolph
4.	Remarks	Dr. Eugene Carson Blake
5.	Tribute to Negro Women Fighters for Freedom	Mrs. Medgar Evers
6.	Remarks	John Lewis
7.	Remarks	Walter Reuther
8.	Remarks	James Farmer
9.	Selection	Eva Jessye
10.	Prayer	Rabbi Uri Miller
11.	Remarks	Whitney M. Young Jr.
12.	Remarks	Mathew Ahmann
13.	Remarks	Roy Wilkins
14.	Selection	Miss Mahalia Jackson
15.	Remarks	Rabbi Joachim Prinz
16.	Remarks	The Rev. Dr. Martin Luther King Jr.
17.	The Pledge	A. Philip Randolph
18.	Benediction	Dr. Benjamin E. Mays

"WE SHALL OVERCOME"

Joan Baez and Bob Dylan

As the crowd around the monument grew ever larger, a program of music began at 10:00. Joan Baez crooned "Oh Freedom" and "All My Trials Will Soon Be Over." The most popular protest singers of the day were on hand: Odetta; Josh White; Bob Dylan; and Peter, Paul and Mary.

The songs were also approved in advance by Rustin. All were peaceful folk-music ballads about courage. Peter, Paul and Mary sang "Blowin' in the Wind" and "If I Had a Hammer."

Peter, Paul and Mary

Hollywood Stars

Many stars in Hollywood actively supported the civil rights movement. Present that day were black actors such as Sidney Poitier, Harry Belafonte, Sammy Davis Jr., Ossie Davis, and Ruby Dee. There were white actors, too, including Paul Newman, Joanne Woodward, Charlton Heston, Marlon Brando, Dennis Hopper, and Tony Curtis. Teen singing idol Bobby Darin announced that he was "proud, and kind of choked up."

Sidney Poitier

One famous African American entertainer, Josephine Baker, had flown in from France. She told everyone, "You can't go wrong. The world is behind you."

The first black airline stewardess took the microphone. It was Ruth Carol Taylor, who in 1957, as part of her training, had learned not to respond to racist insults. She urged everyone to shout "Freedom!" over and over so it could "be heard all over the world."

Glamorous singer Lena Horne later shouted the same word, stretching it out over five seconds. A young witness responded, "Where there had been tension, before I got on the bus, the busyness in my body *settled*. I became so peaceful. People were crying."

At 10:30, an announcement came over the loudspeakers: Ninety thousand people were now gathered. The crowd cheered.

And still trains and buses kept streaming in. A caravan of four hundred fifty buses arrived from Harlem. Other buses came from Chicago, Baltimore, Boston, Detroit, and

Birmingham—all the major cities in the United States. Some small towns sent a single bus. In all, more than two thousand buses, forty trains, ten chartered planes, and countless cars were en route to Washington.

Baseball hero Jackie Robinson was there with his family, as well as Rosa Parks and other heroes of the civil rights movement.

At one point, ten thousand more people were arriving every ten to fifteen minutes. The green of the Mall's lawn was vanishing under the feet of a massive crowd. "Everyone was friendly, sharing, caring . . . singing and laughing," a thirteen-year-old remembered.

Estimates vary, but most put the final count at an astounding two hundred fifty to three hundred thousand people. It was about 70 percent black and 30 percent white. That meant about seventy-five thousand white marchers were there.

The March leaders were glad about that.

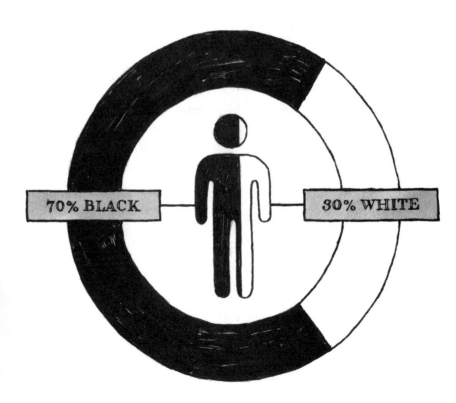

One fifteen-year-old marcher said, "I was so happy to see that in the white people, that they could listen and take in and respect and believe in the words of a black person. I had never seen anything like that."

Another person said, "I was awestruck by the multicolored faces of the marchers: their dedication, their sincerity, their somberness, and their unspoken resolve to make a difference."

At 11:30, the ten leaders of the March were to walk at the head of the crowd to the Lincoln Memorial. But as the time drew near, the leaders were nowhere to be seen. They were stuck in meetings on Capitol Hill.

Eager marchers didn't want to wait. So they started off early, led by a high school marching band in bright yellow jackets.

Rustin almost panicked. He tried to hold people back without success. Quickly, the civil rights leaders were rushed to the scene. Aides made a break in the crowd for the leaders so they could pose as if they were at the very front.

Roy Wilkins of the NAACP looked around at the sea of people and said, "This is the king of all marches!"

CHAPTER 6
Millions of Footsteps

The marchers headed down Constitution and Independence Avenues toward the Lincoln Memorial, one mile away.

"Constitution Avenue is awash with a human river," a marcher named Edward Morgan said when describing the scene later, with "signs for freedom now bobbing like sailboats above the marchers' heads."

This wasn't a parade. The crowd did not march in straight lines. And few people watched from the sidelines. Marchers stayed in groups as many as thirty abreast. Some smiled. Others were crying. Most had serious looks on their faces. Sometimes, all of a sudden, people started chanting—chants like "Jamesey Crow must go!" Some sang, but often only the sound of footsteps was heard.

Many were ordinary people dressed in their Sunday best. Some had never been to DC before and were awestruck. "It was like coming into Rome, with all those marble buildings," said a man from New Jersey.

One foot forward. Another foot forward . . .

Was anyone scared?

Of course.

"There was a real feeling of excitement mixed with anxiety in the air," said a marcher. "There was the feeling that anything could happen to you at any time."

But there was no violence. All police had to do was help people find lost friends and direct vehicles to parking places.

The KKK's Imperial Grand Wizard had vowed to show up. But he had plane trouble and never arrived. The head of the American Nazi Party had planned to bring in ten thousand followers to disrupt the March. He showed up with only a very small group. One of his men was arrested for giving a speech—a hate-filled speech—without a permit, and the Nazi party members left.

Most of the crowd was unaware of this incident. A minister described the mood as "euphoria"— really, really happy. The March was turning out to be what everyone had wished for.

By 2:30, everyone had reached the Lincoln Memorial. For many, that one-mile walk was the most important journey of their lives.

Before the speeches, there was music. An organist started off with "The Battle Hymn of the Republic," a song from the Civil War days. "We Shall Overcome" was the second song. Based on an old hymn about peace and justice, it was made

famous by folksinger Pete Seeger. People would join hands while singing and make up new verses such as, "We are not afraid."

The day got hotter. The temperature rose to 87 degrees. Roasting in the sun, some fanned themselves with their programs or dipped their bare feet into the Lincoln Memorial Reflecting Pool.

Lines for toilets and for food were hundreds of people long. A few fainted from the heat and some were brought to first-aid stations. (These people were lifted above the packed crowd and passed from person to person.) By the end of the day, the Red Cross treated a total of 1,355 people. Just one person died; it was from a heart attack.

Sunlight glinted on the pool, shooting reflections everywhere. A quarter of a million people now waited to hear words that would express why they had come to Washington.

Marian Anderson

The popular black opera star Marian Anderson was supposed to sing the national anthem at the March. But her plane was delayed.

In 1939, she had held a concert of her very own on the steps of the Lincoln Memorial. First Lady Eleanor Roosevelt had arranged it after a white women's group refused to let Anderson appear in their hall.

Marian Anderson's concert was the first in Washington to draw a crowd of both black and white people. Seventy-five thousand came.

Now she was returning to the steps of the Lincoln Memorial. She arrived late, but she was in time to bowl over the crowd with the song "He's Got the Whole World in His Hands."

CHAPTER 7
The Power of Words

Against the white marble background of the Lincoln Memorial, speakers addressed the crowd.

A. Philip Randolph spoke first. The March was the fulfillment of his life's dream. He

congratulated everyone on being part of the "largest demonstration in the history of this nation." He continued, "We are not a mob. We are [here] for jobs and freedom. . . . When we leave, it will be to carry the civil rights revolution home with us."

After Randolph finished, over one hundred members of Congress took their seats on the front steps. Right away, the marchers chanted, "Pass the bill! Pass the bill!"

The importance of JFK's civil rights bill was echoed in other speeches. Roy Wilkins stated that everyone at the March, as well as millions of other Americans, couldn't understand why the government seemed "powerless to prevent the physical abuse of its citizens within its own borders." Laws had to protect black people—civil rights laws.

One particular speaker worried the organizers. His name was John Lewis. At twenty-three, he

was the youngest speaker. The speech he first planned to use refused to support JFK's bill because he felt it was a case of too little, too late. It had no protection against police brutality, for example. One line in Lewis's speech was, "To those who have said, 'Be patient and wait,' we must say that *patience* is a dirty and nasty word." John Lewis wanted change fast. He was the leader of the Student Nonviolent Coordinating Committee and had taken part in many sit-ins and protests. Afraid that this speech would spark a riot, some other speakers said they would not appear unless Lewis made changes.

Randolph had persuaded Lewis to tone down his words. The night before the March, Lewis rewrote his speech in his hotel room. Less than an hour before he came before the crowd, he was still working on it in a janitor's closet underneath the Lincoln statue. Finally, it was finished and typed.

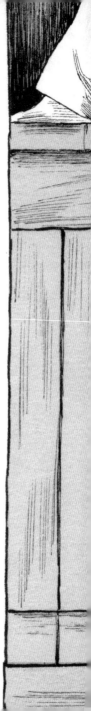

Just in case Lewis became too fiery or it looked like the crowd would turn angry, someone from the Justice Department was on hand to cut his microphone and go to a soothing Mahalia Jackson recording.

When John Lewis took the stage, he began hesitantly, his voice cracking. The speech was toned down but still strong, urging immediate passage of the bill. Otherwise, he promised more marches in more cities "with the spirit of love and with the spirit of dignity that we have shown here today." He ended by saying, "We must say, wake up, America, wake up! For we cannot stop, and we will not and cannot be patient."

The crowd interrupted him fourteen times with applause. Lewis said later, "The speech still had fire. It still had bite."

As the afternoon went on, there were more speeches. Were there any white speakers?

Yes.

Mahalia Jackson

Mahalia Jackson was a popular black gospel singer who was at the March. Gospel songs are religious songs, songs about Jesus. Eight million copies of her recording of "Move On Up a Little Higher" were sold.

A longtime friend of the King family, Jackson would sing to Martin Luther King Jr. over the phone when he got discouraged about civil rights.

Walter Reuther, head of a powerful union for automobile workers, gave one of the speeches. He had marched with civil rights groups in Mississippi and was a friend of Martin Luther King Jr.'s. He said, "We cannot successfully preach democracy in the world unless we first practice democracy at home. . . . It is the responsibility of every American to share the impatience of the Negro American."

Did any women give major speeches at the March?

No.

At one point, Daisy Bates, a longtime activist, read a list called "Tribute to Negro Women Fighters for Freedom." Rosa Parks, who was at the Lincoln Memorial that day, was among the women honored. She stood but didn't speak. She had not been asked to. A woman who worked for Rustin felt "embarrassed." After all, black women were crucial to the civil rights movement. The leaders' poor excuse was that they were afraid that by picking one woman to give a major speech, others would be jealous.

The final speech of the day was from thirty-four-year-old Martin Luther King Jr. He was such a great speaker that no one wanted to follow him. He had learned from his father, a famous preacher. He had taken many classes in public speaking and practiced sermons in front of a mirror. In 1963 alone, he made more than three hundred fifty speeches all over the United States.

But now his speech was being televised to a

national audience, and he was under pressure. How could he sum up this historic day? King had been working all night. Now the final typed speech was in front of him.

At 3:30, Randolph introduced King as "the moral leader of our nation." The applause went on for a full minute.

In his rich, deep voice, King began by reminding America of its many broken promises to blacks. Racial prejudice was not just morally wrong, he maintained, it was un-American. He understood black people's anger, most of all those who had been beaten or jailed for standing up for

their rights. Still, he encouraged nonviolence and a spirit of love for one's enemies.

The crowd gave him their full attention.

From a few feet away, his friend Mahalia Jackson piped up, "Tell them about the dream, Martin. *Please*, tell them about the dream!"

King had been talking about a dream of his for months. Some of his aides thought he'd been overusing it. Now he turned over his prepared text and began to speak from the heart. "I have a dream," he declared.

He began to describe a future where blacks and whites lived together in peace. His dream was a bold one, but not a fantasy. He wanted people to see it as real and true.

The more he repeated, "I have a dream," the more powerful it grew. "I have a dream that my four little children will one day live in a nation where they will not be judged by the color of their skin but by the content of their character."

Even in places like Alabama, he predicted, "little black boys and black girls will be able to join hands with little white boys and white girls as sisters and brothers."

His language was biblical, poetic, and gorgeous. He ended by calling on people to go home and keep working toward this dream so that someday all Americans would be free.

King's words wrapped up the entire day with a powerful message of hope. He went way over his time limit—his speech ran a total of sixteen minutes—but no one cared. By the end, everyone was crying, smiling, or both. Strangers were hugging one another.

JFK, watching on his TV at the White House, was awed. So were Americans all over the country. In fact, thanks to the new satellite technology of Telstar, King's speech was broadcast live around the world.

Some thought his speech was not demanding enough. It was too nice. Others were outraged by his vision of blacks and whites living together as equals. John Williams, a representative of Mississippi, later called King the "most notorious gangster of our generation."

But most thought the speech was a masterpiece, one that ranked alongside Lincoln's Gettysburg Address in expressing the best hopes of America.

CHAPTER 8
"We Shall Overcome"

By now "everybody was all used up," said Mahalia Jackson.

After King's speech, Randolph was weeping, calling this "the most beautiful and glorious day of my life."

He was too speechless to give concluding remarks, so Bayard Rustin got his chance to speak. He presented a list of ten basic ways to desegregate all areas of American life. Each one was met with a roar of approval from the crowd.

The day ended ahead of schedule at 4:15. Linking arms, people sang "We Shall Overcome" one more time.

Buses and trains were already revving up their engines, ready to take the marchers home.

The civil rights leaders left for their meeting with President Kennedy. At the White House, there was coffee, sandwiches, and cherry cobbler. For nearly an hour, JFK and his vice president, Lyndon Johnson, talked with the leaders about the civil rights bill.

Already there was the sense that the March had helped to put the civil rights movement on the national map.

The next day, the *New York Herald Tribune* called it "a great day in American history" and "a national high-water mark in mass decency." It touched many who hadn't given civil rights much thought. Especially white people. As a government official said, "It moved an awful lot of citizens who were very indifferent to realizing there's something that has to be done."

Yet just over two weeks later, a black church in Birmingham was bombed. Four young girls were killed.

What about JFK's bill? Opponents were able to stall it in committee, delaying its passage time and again.

Then on November 22, 1963, President John F. Kennedy was shot and killed as he rode in an open limo past cheering crowds in Dallas, Texas.

The hopeful day of the March already seemed a part of the distant past.

But the new president, Lyndon Johnson, promised to follow through with the bill. He did. The following July he signed the Civil Rights Act of 1964—less than a year after the March.

This, combined with the Voting Rights Act of 1965, which promised government enforcement of voting rights, represented the official end of Jim Crow.

Three years later, the Civil Rights Act of 1968 was signed. This made it illegal to refuse to sell a house in a white neighborhood to a black person.

President Lyndon Johnson

It was another great moment in the cause of equality. But the event came at a sad time. The act was signed into law by President Johnson one week after Martin Luther King Jr. was shot to death as he stood on his hotel balcony in Memphis, Tennessee.

If only King had lived to see Barack Obama take office as the first African American president of the United States on January 20, 2009. Yet even though King was dead, his dream had lived on.

"When people stand up and make up their minds to move and take action," said a twenty-year-old marcher, "it opens doors."

Today in the United States, people are still treated unfairly because of their gender or religion or the color of their skin. Every door that is opened meets with resistance.

But the doors open, anyway.

Timeline of the March on Washington

1941 — A. Philip Randolph first proposes a march on Washington against discrimination in January

— On June 25, President Franklin Delano Roosevelt creates the Fair Employment Practices Committee and Randolph calls off the proposed march on Washington

1961 — President John F. Kennedy is sworn into office

1962 — A. Philip Randolph and Bayard Rustin begin to plan the 1963 March on Washington

1963 — The March on Washington for Jobs and Freedom occurs on August 28

— The Sixteenth Street Baptist Church in Birmingham is bombed, killing four African American girls, on September 15

— President John F. Kennedy is assassinated on November 22

1964 — Congress passes the Civil Rights Act of 1964, which bans racial discrimination in public places

1965 — Congress passes the Voting Rights Act, outlawing discriminatory voting practices, on August 6

1968 — Martin Luther King Jr. is assassinated on April 4

— Congress passes the Civil Rights Act of 1968, ending housing discrimination, on April 11

— Robert F. Kennedy is assassinated on June 5

Timeline of the World

World War II ends after the nuclear bombing of Hiroshima and Nagasaki	1945
The Vietnam War begins	1955
The Beatles form in Liverpool	1960
Construction of the Berlin Wall begins	1961
The Soviet Union sends the first man into outer space on April 12	
Programming language BASIC is invented	1964
The Cultural Revolution in China begins, causing social and political upheaval	1966
The Six-Day War is fought between Israel and its neighboring states	1967
Che Guevara is executed in Bolivia on October 9	
President Richard Nixon elected	1968
The Stonewall Riots signal the start of the gay rights movement in the United States	1969
Neil Armstrong becomes the first man to step on the moon on July 20	

Bibliography

*Books for young readers

Alexander, Michelle. *The New Jim Crow: Mass Incarceration in the Age of Colorblindness*. NY: The New Press, 2010.

Barber, Lucy G. *Marching on Washington: The Forging of an American Political Tradition*. Berkeley: University of California Press, 2002.

Bass, Patrik Henry. *Like a Mighty Stream: The March on Washington, August 28, 1963*. Philadelphia: Running Press, 2002.

* Bartoletti, Susan Campbell. *They Called Themselves the K.K.K.: The Birth of an American Terrorist Group*. NY: Houghton Mifflin, 2010.

* Brimner, Larry Dane. *We Are One: The Story of Bayard Rustin*. Honesdale, PA: Calkins Creek, 2007.

Euchner, Charles. *Nobody Turn Me Around: A People's History of the 1963 March on Washington*. Boston: Beacon Press, 2010.

Gates, Henry Louis. *Life Upon These Shores: Looking at African American History*, 1513–2008. NY: Knopf, 2011.

Hansen, Drew D. *The Dream: Martin Luther King, Jr., and the Speech that Inspired a Nation*. NY: Ecco, 2003.

Jones, Clarence B. and Stuart Connelly. *Behind the Dream: The Making of the Speech that Transformed a Nation*. NY: Macmillan, 2011.

King, Coretta Scott. *My Life with Martin Luther King, Jr*. New York: Holt, Rinehart and Winston, 1969.

* Levinson, Cynthia. *We've Got a Job: The 1963 Birmingham Children's March*. Atlanta, GA: Peachtree, 2012.

Marable, Manning and Leith Mullings. *Freedom: A Photographic History of the African American Struggle*. NY: Phaidon, 2002.

* McWhorter, Diane. *A Dream of Freedom: The Civil Rights Movement from 1954 to 1968*. NY: Scholastic, 2004.

* Miller, Jake. *The 1963 March on Washington: Speeches and Songs for Civil Rights*. NY: Rosen Publishing, 2004.

* Osborne, Linda Barrett. *Miles to Go for Freedom: Segregation and Civil Rights in the Jim Crow Years*. NY: Abrams, 2012.

Podair, Jerald E. *Bayard Rustin: American Dreamer*. MD: Rowman and Littlefield, 2009.

Williams, Juan. *Eyes on the Prize: America's Civil Rights Years, 1954–1965*. NY: Penguin, 1988.

Woodward, C. Vann. *The Strange Career of Jim Crow*, third edition. NY: Oxford University Press, 1974.

YOUR HEADQUARTERS FOR HISTORY

Activities, Mad Libs, and sidesplitting jokes!
Discover the Who HQ books beyond the biographies